Original title:
Tales from the Tesseract

Copyright © 2025 Creative Arts Management OÜ
All rights reserved.

Author: Helena Marchant
ISBN HARDBACK: 978-1-80567-796-3
ISBN PAPERBACK: 978-1-80567-917-2

Flickers in the Ethereal Divide

In a blink, the cat danced, oh so spry,
Wearing socks that defied all time and sky.
A toaster rebelled, made a toast of cheese,
While jellybeans giggled in zigzag breeze.

Chasing shadows on the wall so bright,
The lamp pulled a prank, flickered with delight.
A polka-dotted fish taught a waltz to flies,
As squirrels in suits debated cake and pies.

Essence of the Interstellar Rift

A noodle flew past, with a wink and a grin,
Claiming spaghetti was the key to win.
A sofa set sail on a river of ink,
While the fridge sang songs, made the neighbors blink.

Balloons in the sky held a grand parade,
Where cupcakes swapped tales, and laughter played.
A merry-go-round spun with socks and shoes,
In realms where giggles unravel the blues.

Tales of the Zero-Point Field

A jellybean comet zipped by with flair,
Tickling the stars, it danced in the air.
The clocks were confused, ticking backward with glee,
While marshmallows floated like clouds on a spree.

A kit from the cupboard, oh what a sight,
Baking up dreams throughout the long night.
Where whispers of nonsense made the cosmos shake,
The quarks joined a band, with a drum and a cake.

Eclipsed Horizons of Memory

A goat in a top hat recited a play,
To forks and spoons who giggled all day.
The sun wore a frown, painted in hues,
While rainboots danced in a jolly ol' blues.

A fish had a conversation with pie,
As clouds debated on how high they could fly.
The tales grew sillier, in a twist upon twist,
In the land of the absurd where nothing's missed.

The Symmetry of Spectral Echoes

In a world where shadows play,
A cat wears glasses, night and day.
Two left feet dance with no proud grace,
As mirrors laugh, they show the face.

Wobbling cubes on a bumpy ride,
Juggling stars like an awkward guide.
A polka dot worm debates the moon,
While giggles rumble, a soaring tune.

Archways to Alternate Dimensions

Through a door that spins and twirls,
I find a land of silly squirrels.
They wear tiny hats and sing aloud,
While juggling acorns, feeling proud.

A bridge made out of candy canes,
Leads to lands where logic wanes.
Puddles sprout with dancing fish,
Hopping high with every swish.

Secrets of the Spatial Fabric

In a closet where socks conspire,
Lies a kingdom built on yarn and fire.
Knitting needles twist and kite,
Creating worlds as day turns night.

A plush unicorn in a top hat,
Makes tea with a singing acrobat.
They toast to dreams, both wild and free,
In a space that smiles, just wait and see.

Delving into the Dimensional Deep

A snail plays chess with a wise old tree,
Who claims he's good – just wait and see!
As bubbles pop from out of space,
A game of laughter takes first place.

In a whirlpool full of spaghetti,
Dancing forks are always ready.
They twirl and spin, a festive ball,
In a landscape where fun is for all.

Lost Echoes of the Multiverse

In a world of skewed reflections,
Laughter bends at funny angles.
A cat in boots steals all connections,
While a butterfly forms jangles.

Quantum bits in frocks and hats,
Joking with a cosmic twist.
A rabbit sings alongside the cats,
As galaxies join in the list.

With every jump, a new surprise,
Wormholes laugh at space and time.
While cosmic clowns juggle the skies,
Echoes dance, a silly rhyme.

So let us dance in whimsy's jest,
With every bounce, a giggly cheer.
In the multiverse, we're all blessed,
Laughter's whispers, bright and clear.

Songs of Time's Infinite Weave

Tick-tock goes the wobbly clock,
While socks in pairs roam free.
Ludicrous tunes from a dozing rock,
Spin stories with glee, oh me!

Beavers building time machines,
Wearing spectacles, what a sight!
Singing rhymes with crop-top jeans,
As clocks dance in the moonlight.

Paradoxes join the parade,
Wobbling whims in a curvy line.
History's missed, but not dismayed,
Each note is a silly sign.

So clap your hands, embrace the joke,
As hickory sticks begin to play.
Time's tapestry of threads bespoke,
Woven laughter lights the way.

Navigating the Unseen Dimensions

Wormholes giggle in corners tight,
As dimensions jump and spin.
A squirrel with wings takes flight,
Chasing rainbows with a grin.

Maps drawn in butter, hard to read,
With arrows that lead to nowhere.
A compass spins in fervent speed,
As we tumble through cosmic air.

Frogs in tuxedos navigate,
Through portals to whimsical lands.
Each twist and turn, a chance to skate,
On shimmering strands of rubber bands.

So pack your joy, let's take a ride,
Where unseen worlds tickle the mind.
In dimensions wide, we shall abide,
With laughter's echo intertwined.

Whirlwinds of Fate in a Celestial Dance

In a disco ball of stars so bright,
Planets twist in silly prance.
Galactic zippers zip with delight,
As comets twirl in a dance.

Asteroids wear funky shoes,
While solar flares drape in style.
Dancing to the cosmic blues,
Laughing all the while.

Fate flips cards beneath her dress,
With jokers wild in every round.
Round and round, no time to stress,
In the whirlwind's laughter found.

So spin and sway with grace so bold,
As galaxies join the whimsical chance.
In celestial realms, let stories unfold,
With whirlwinds of fate in this dance.

Secrets of the Quantum Veil

In a world of odd whispers, I found a strange cat,
It spoke in riddles while wearing a hat.
I pondered its secrets, all tangled and bright,
An equation for dinner, a theorem for night.

With particles dancing in chaotically neat,
I laughed as they wobbled, two left feet.
They giggled and twirled, oh what a delight,
Making math seem so silly, defying the night.

Journeys Beyond the Known

I hopped on a comet, grabbed a bright star,
We raced through the cosmos, oh so bizarre.
The Moon played guitar while Mars sang a tune,
The asteroids chuckled, all mad in their swoon.

We served tea to aliens who loved a good pun,
While quarks played hopscotch in beams of the sun.
The travels were wild, a splendid fun spree,
Each planet we'd visit laughed heartily with glee.

Threads of Fate in a Bending Space

In a fabric of time that wrinkled and glowed,
I lost my left sock, where could it have flowed?
The universe giggled, its seams all a-crackle,
As I chased through dimensions, a silly debacle.

Each thread that I pulled, a tale spun anew,
A sock puppet joined, as we twirled and flew.
With each knot and tangle, our laughter unfurled,
In the stitches of fate, we twirled and whirled.

The Echo Chamber of Lost Realities

In a room full of echoes where voices collide,
I found my own laughter, it tried to hide.
Each bounce brought a smile, a pet rock found a friend,
In a maze of reflections, the giggles won't end.

We played peek-a-boo with dimensions unknown,
As realities flipped like a well-tossed stone.
We juggled the shadows, a comedic ballet,
In the chamber of echoes, we danced night and day.

The Color of Infinity's Eye

In a world where rainbows glow,
The colors dance, a lively show.
Purple cats in hats parade,
While upside-down, the trees cascade.

A polka-dot sun beams with glee,
Kites that fly from C to Z.
Silly fish wear clownish smiles,
As bouncing kangaroos run miles.

Every shade has a voice to tell,
Of funny jokes in a color well.
They giggle as they spin and swirl,
In the cosmic wind, they whirl.

So if you ever find a hue,
Remember all the laughs it drew.
Just peek into infinity's eye,
Where every glance is bound to fly.

Fragments of an Infinite Story

Once upon a time, they say,
A pickle ruled a grand buffet.
With toast as knights in armor bright,
They battled crumbs with all their might.

A donut wore a crown of sprinkles,
While marshmallows did jump and twinkle.
From pages torn, the tales would leap,
In a land where cookies never sleep.

They danced on clouds of whipped cream fluff,
And shouted, 'This is sure enough!'
Fragments of giggles filled the air,
As silly stories danced with flair.

Each chapter ends with laughter loud,
As jellybeans form a cheering crowd.
They weave a tale, both strange and bright,
With snippets of pure, fun delight.

Beyond the Event Horizon

A rocket ship made out of cheese,
Zooms through space with silly ease.
It hovers near a burger star,
And wishes on a candy bar.

Past galaxies of gummy bears,
With comet trails of marshmallow flares.
The universe sings a funny tune,
Where jokesters bounce on the moon.

Black holes yawn in lazy ways,
While astronauts share nutty plays.
They toss around the cosmic pie,
And watch the beans do backflips high.

In this realm where giggles reign,
Even the aliens join the train.
A ride through laughter, bright and bold,
Beyond horizons, stories unfold.

The Luminary's Journey Through Shadows

A lightbulb ventured through the dusk,
In search of spark and fun robust.
With photons dancing at each bend,
A sunny joke could be a trend.

Through darkened nooks, it flipped the switch,
And shadows laughed, not a single glitch.
With beam and giggle, it would glow,
Making darkness just a show.

The owls hooted, 'What a sight!'
As shadows twirled with pure delight.
They played hide-and-seek in style,
Making even dusk break into smile.

At last, it found the brightest hue,
In every corner, laughter grew.
A luminary's path, so bright and true,
In shadows, found a funny crew.

Rhapsodies from the Beyond

In a realm where socks escape,
The laundry folds into a drape.
A cat plays chess with space-time,
Laughing hard, it claims each crime.

The toaster sings a jazzy tune,
While bread does a funky swoon.
The clock, it ticks in backward gait,
As squirrels conspire, plotting fate.

A bike rides up a spiral stair,
To find a dance party in thin air.
With wobbling moves, they join the cha-cha,
As gravity hides 'neath the colorful flora.

When pancakes float through pastel skies,
The syrup dreams of endless pies.
In laughter, worlds collide and spread,
As joy booms loud—no tears to shed.

The Transitory Nature of Space

In galaxies where bubbles burst,
A porcupine makes pasta first.
With aliens that love to groan,
They borrow cosmic spoons, then moan.

An astronaut found cheese on Mars,
Declaring it the planet's stars.
With each bite, a comet flies,
As laughter echoes through the skies.

Jellybeans shaped like a cloud,
Grumpy robots, buzzing loud.
They sipped their tea in zero g,
While upside-down, they learned to flee.

A quasar wears a floppy hat,
Baking muffins with a spunky cat.
Together they mix stardust sprinkles,
Spinning tales with laughter's twinkles.

Explorations Beyond the Expanse

In a ship made of chocolate bars,
We sailed past glittering stars.
Navigating under cotton candy,
With music from a robot bandy.

Strawberry comets raced the moon,
While penguins danced a silly tune.
They slipped and slid on rings of gold,
With stories of the brave and bold.

A fish in space wore roller skates,
Casting nets with jelly straits.
He caught a burger, set it free,
Said, "You'll never catch me, see!"

As planets giggle and wink around,
We explore the weird, the profound.
In laughter, we drift through night,
Chasing dreams of pure delight.

Reflections in a Fractal Mirror

In a mirror of patterns, I smile,
Each crackle and twinkle beguile.
I ponder my face, a silly disguise,
Made of cupcakes and floating pies.

A double take left me awestruck,
My doppelgänger? Oh, what luck!
He ordered a pizza, I chose a cake,
In this world, we both just partake.

Reflections twist in dizzying loops,
I wave at the gathering goofs.
A parade of me, with wobbly grace,
Trying to dance in the same place.

Yet, echoes of laughter collide,
With every step, we cannot hide.
We trip and tumble, a humorous plight,
In a kaleidoscopic, endless light.

Navigating the Space Between

Between the realms where oddities bloom,
Lies a path that leads to the room.
A cat with a hat, and a dog on a bike,
They argue what snacks they both like.

I slipped through a crack with a grin,
Where rubber chickens merrily spin.
Floating on marshmallows, I took a ride,
Balancing jellybeans, my newfound guide.

I found the map upside-down,
Marked with places where they all drown
In puddles of giggles and quirky sips,
Joy spilled over from whimsical lips.

As I navigated with flair and sass,
I wondered if I'd ever pass.
In the space between, the fun won't cease,
Each wrong turn just brings me more peace.

Harmonies of Colliding Universes

In the fabric of space, a joke unspooled,
Planets collide and giggle, oh so ruled.
A fish on a scooter sings alien tunes,
While cows waltz beneath the cartoon moons.

I caught a glimpse of a starry sight,
Two worlds tangoed in chaotic flight.
With harmonies blending, an odd ballet,
Who knew planets could dance in such play?

Every collision brings laughter's cheer,
A symphony played for all who can hear.
Galactic choirs of comical prose,
Unruly notes where the laughter grows.

The cosmos smiles with every twist,
In these universes, you can't resist.
With jokes from the stars and puns on the spin,
It's music for those who dare to grin.

The Cartographer's Guide to Parallel Lives

A map unraveled, with lines so bent,
Showing lives that mischievously went.
One version of me takes tea with a bear,
While another builds rockets in mid-air.

I charted a course through whimsical lands,
With crayon scribbles and cookie hands.
Each version of me a dizzying sight,
One juggles pancakes, another takes flight.

In this atlas of zany delight,
Every fork leads to endless laughs at night.
With paths that twisted and turns oh so wide,
Who knew I had kids, and a pet, and a bride?

As I navigate my own crazy spree,
I find comedy, with every 'me.'
In the map of existence, such laughter thrives,
In the cartographer's guide to parallel lives.

The Dance of Divergent Dimensions

In a realm where oddities prance,
Dimensions twist and foam like a dance.
A square tried to waltz with a line,
But they tripped on a circle, oh, what a sign!

Bubbles of color flipped through the air,
A triangle shouted, "All's fair!"
In this jittery jig of space and time,
The jabberwock laughed, oh, how sublime!

With every twist, a giggle would grow,
As the clock tangled up, too fast to slow.
A wormhole hiccupped, spilled out jellybeans,
While gravity sucked up all the machines.

So come join the chaos, dance without fright,
In dimensions where logic takes flight.
For in this paradox, laughter's the key,
Unlocking the door to our jubilee!

Enigmas of the Infinite Echo

In a canyon where echoes grow wide,
A joke told twice took a curious ride.
It bounced off walls, then back to my ear,
Diagnosis: laughter! Everyone cheer!

The mountains giggled, the valleys replied,
The universe chuckling, a cosmic guide.
With every riddle wrapped in a plot,
The answers played hide and seek, oh what a lot!

Whispers of nonsense drift through the trees,
As squirrels debate with the cosmic breeze.
Each puzzle a giggle, every mystery bright,
In this vast echo, all wrongs feel right.

So ponder the echoes, both silly and grand,
In this giggling void, hand in hand.
For every enigma, there's laughter in store,
Infinite echoes that always want more!

Secrets in the Spacetime Tangle

In the fabric of space, a knot just appears,
Time plays the fiddles; it's all filled with cheers.
A sock lost in laundry, a mystery rife,
Hides secrets and giggles; oh, what a life!

Chrono-kittens bound through loops of their tail,
Chasing past futures, leaving behind a trail.
The watch tick-tocked jokes over dimensions unseen,
While a pencil scribbled all the words in between.

Bubbles of time popped in bright colors of fun,
As clocks played tag under the smiling sun.
The secret's revealed with a chuckle and grin,
In the spacetime tangle, the laughter begins!

So unravel the threads, let the laughter unfold,
In this tangled up world where nothing's too bold.
For secrets of joy are for all to embrace,
In the dance of dimensions, we all find our place!

Celestial Serenades and the Past

Stars strum guitars in the cosmic ballet,
Singing of stories from eons away.
The moon took a bow, the sun did a twirl,
As comets danced past with a giggling swirl.

Each planet chimed in with its own silly tune,
While asteroids juggled beneath the bright moon.
The Milky Way laughed with a shimmering star,
As echoes of laughter drifted near and far.

Time travelers pranced through their journeys of light,
Each one a giggle, a fun-filled sight.
With memories wrapped in a cosmic embrace,
They spun tales of joy in this endless space.

So pull up a chair, join this celestial choir,
Where past meets the present, and hearts catch fire.
For in this universe of laughter and cheer,
The serenades echo, reminding us to steer!

Visions Beyond the Veil of Reality

In a world where pigeons wear bows,
And squirrels exchange stocks and shows.
A cat took a train to tour the moon,
While singing a tune with a plastic spoon.

Mirrors laugh at your shoes, so bright,
While shadows dance in the pale moonlight.
A fish rode a bike, what a sight!
It waved to the cat, dressed in white.

The trees tell jokes, they crack up the breeze,
With roots that trip on playful knees.
Clouds are the chefs, serving up dreams,
With rain that tastes like strawberry creams.

Watch out for the sun, it may play tricks,
With rays that tickle like feathered picks.
In this realm of giggles and glee,
You'll find life's laughter is the key.

Chronicles of the Celestial Weavers

The stars in the sky spin tales of yarn,
While moons strut around with an air of charm.
A tapestry stitched with hiccuping light,
And a warp of wonders that dance in the night.

Silly spiders weave clouds into hats,
While cosmic kittens chase after bats.
The universe giggles, a cheeky sprite,
With a punchline that teeters on edge of night.

Saturn's rings juggle planets at play,
While comets slide by in a graceful ballet.
Everyone's laughing as gravity bends,
In this cosmic circus where nonsense descends.

But hold on tight, do not lose your seat,
For the riddles of space are a curious treat.
So let's take a stroll through this curious land,
Where humor and chaos go hand in hand.

Reflections in the Fourth Dimension

In the fourth dimension, it's hard to align,
With mirrors that giggle and tickle your spine.
A dog plays chess with a wise old frog,
While time takes a breather, wrapped in a fog.

The clocks play hopscotch, each tick out of tune,
As the sun takes a nap beneath a bright moon.
Chasing its tail, a funny old ghost,
Whispers the jokes that we love the most.

Dimensions collide in a whimsical dance,
Inviting the curious to join in the prance.
Twisted reflections, all silly and bright,
Bring laughter and joy through the cloak of the night.

So grab a dimension, twist it just right,
As we step through the fun into whimsical flight.
With giggles unbound in this space-time parade,
The laughter we share, a memory made.

The Echoes of Infinite Worlds

In a world where bananas wear tiny hats,
And frogs can tell tales of curious chats.
With laughter that echoes through valleys and hills,
Where humor dissolves all your worries and thrills.

The mountains nod slowly, their peaks made of cheese,
As clouds tumble down, carrying giggling bees.
In this land of delight, where whimsy resides,
The silliness flows like the fun-loving tides.

Each echo a story of laughter and cheer,
Past universes whisper ideas, so dear.
A fumble, a tumble, let's laugh till we cry,
As the echoes of worlds fill the sweet sky.

So come gather round, with imaginations wide,
In the realm of the funny, let joy be your guide.
For the echoes of laughter are bridges unseen,
Connecting us all in this whimsical dream.

Musings from the Multi-Layered Sphere

In a world where socks play hide and seek,
A cat wore a hat and started to speak.
Jellybeans danced on the ceiling up high,
As giggles exploded, like popcorn in the sky.

Two spoons held a race across the old floor,
While pickle and mustard declared an uproar.
Chasing their dreams like they're late for a date,
They spun in circles, oh what a fate!

Caught in a wedgie, a couch cushion sighed,
As marshmallow clouds floated, happily fried.
A pickle in pajamas played chess with a toad,
While laughter erupted, laughter overflowed.

Unicorns trotted with glittery hooves,
Dancing on rainbows, oh how it soothes.
With every layer, a new giggle appears,
In this silly sphere, we'll forget all our fears.

Divergence in the Dimension of Dreams

In a realm where sandwiches argue and brawl,
A cupcake in slippers answered the call.
Dreams twisted around like a pretzel so fine,
As rabbits told jokes over bottles of wine.

A turtle on roller skates zoomed down the lane,
Chasing a duck who sang songs of disdain.
A spoon played the harp while a pie took a bow,
In this wild world, you just never know how.

Underneath blankets of marshmallow fluff,
Were whispers of gummy bears, sweet and tough.
Each dream spun around, a merry-go-round,
Creating a circus where joy could be found.

With laughter as currency, they all gathered near,
In this dimension, there's nothing to fear.
So when you wake up, remember the dance,
For in dreams, dear friend, life's one big prance.

Realms of the Resounding Heart

A frog in a suit gave a speech at the fair,
While lollipops giggled without a single care.
He spoke of big dreams, of jellybean trees,
As butterflies whirled like a sweet, buzzing breeze.

In a land where the clocks moved backward in time,
A blender made smoothies that could sing in rhyme.
Doughnut-shaped planets spun laughter around,
In this quirky realm, pure joy could be found.

With sneakers on giraffes, they leaped through the air,
Chasing the shadows of whimsical flair.
The heartstrings of laughter, all played in a chord,
As confetti of memories danced and ached, adored.

Mirth echoed warmly, like a cinnamon pie,
While rubber ducks floated, just waiting to fly.
In this resounding realm, let your spirit soar,
For love makes the world and laughter makes more.

The Quest for the Cosmic Key

Two pickles and an egg set off with delight,
In search of a key that glimmered so bright.
They traveled through rain with a sidekick named Fred,
A potato who juggled while spinning his head.

Across cosmic paths, they encountered a ghost,
Who ran a café and was quite the good host.
With tea made of stardust and laughter galore,
He served tiny cupcakes that danced on the floor.

Through valleys of jelly and mountains of cream,
Their quest turned to fun, like a wild, silly dream.
The key turned out to be just a grand joke,
For the laughter they shared was the true cosmic cloak.

In the end, they found not a lock to explore,
But a friendship that opened way more than before.
So remember, dear friend, on your own silly spree,
It's love and a smile that unlocks the key!

Starbound Legends and Lunar Lore

In a town where stars would play,
A cow jumped up to steal the day.
The moon just chuckled, spun around,
And laughed at how the cow was crowned.

Galactic frogs had dancing shoes,
They boogied hard, they'd never lose.
Planets swayed, they joined the funk,
A meteor said, 'Let's raise a junk!'

Space elves pranked the Milky Way,
By sending comets out to sway.
A wormhole twisted into a grin,
And whispered, 'Let the fun begin!'

With rockets strapped like silly hats,
They rode the waves of cosmic chats.
In laughter's grip, the cosmos spun,
Creating jokes for everyone!

Unfolding the Fabric of Existence

In a realm where socks can float,
A toaster tried to build a boat.
With buttered bread as its main sail,
They set off through a cosmic trail.

Each planet tossed a dish or two,
While aliens cheered for the crew.
A space cat stretched, then did a flip,
And laughed out loud at their odd trip.

The universe, a patchwork quilt,
With missing pieces, all created guilt.
Yet laughter rang through cosmic night,
As things went wrong, they felt just right!

In zany ways, they shaped the stars,
With giggles shared on Martian cars.
Imagination flew so high,
Even socks could reach the sky!

The Enigma of Cosmic Overlaps

In curves where planets twirled around,
The space fleas danced upon the ground.
With each misstep, they'd leap and fly,
Defying gravity with a cry!

A nebula sprouted a giant grin,
Spinning tales of where they've been.
Galactic squirrels played hide and seek,
While starbursts hummed a tune so chic.

In wormholes, they sought treasures bold,
Like flaming hats and jackets gold.
Each overlap birthed a giggle or two,
Where mysteries spun, like crazy glue!

With universes merging for a jest,
Each whimsy faced an oddball test.
Through twinkling beckons, all would blend,
Creating laughs that never end!

Reverberations from Alternate Horizons

In worlds where rabbits wore bow ties,
And sang of whiskers and moonlit pies.
Alternate realms with wacky fun,
Where ducks would race at the speed of sun.

Each horizon pulsed with silly pranks,
As trees would dance with shaky flanks.
They juggled apples, spun 'round the sun,
A carnival of laughter had just begun.

With every laugh, the cosmos swayed,
In shades of joy, the fears delayed.
In alternate truths, the zany grew,
A endless comedy, forever new!

As echoes rang from every star,
They painted dreams of who they are.
Together bound by cosmic cheer,
In endless realms, they danced with beer!

The Vortex of Variations

In a swirl of socks that dance away,
The carpet giggles, come what may.
A cat in a hat throws glitter galore,
As the floor tiles plot to start a poor war.

Knocking on wood, the chairs decide,
To rumble and tumble, they won't abide.
A clock with arms just can't keep still,
Tick-tock goes the prankster's skill.

Bright polka dots chase a frown,
While the lightbulbs flicker and wear a crown.
"Catch me if you can!" shouts the sly couch,
As cushions conspire to stage a pouch.

Through the space of giggles they float and swirl,
In a patchwork world, where chaos will twirl.
Each twist and turn plays a sneaky game,
A riddle unfolds, who's to take the blame?

Biomimicry of the Infinite

In a bubble where fish wear hats with pride,
And octopuses dance with a confident glide.
The lemons converse with the wise old trees,
While noodles debate if they're meant to please.

A horse whispers secrets to a curious snail,
As rainbows giggle, creating a trail.
"Why don't you mimic me?" a beetle declares,
"Let's twirl in the air with our whimsical pairs!"

The flowers all mimic each other's pose,
As dragons play tag with the friendly crows.
Bouncing through time on the back of a frog,
Wishing on stars made of whipped cream and fog.

All creatures unite in this curious game,
Where nothing is serious, yet all's just the same.
Laugh lines form patterns in each silly scene,
As nature's own jesters dance in between.

The Chalice of Celestial Stories

Under a moon that winks just right,
Sip from the chalice of pure delight.
Stars bounce around, trading their tales,
While comets bring cookies in variegated pails.

A sunbeam steals gossip from clouds on high,
As the cosmos chuckles, oh my, oh my!
The planets play poker, with rings all aglow,
Shooting stars shout, "Who's next in the show?"

Galaxies swarm like bees in the hive,
Sharing their secrets of how to thrive.
Saturn's got jokes that would make you fall,
While Jupiter juggles like he's having a ball.

In a universe filled with laughter and cheer,
The chalice is brimming with stories sincere.
So raise up your cup to these celestial fun,
For each giggle ignites, and we're never done!

Chromatic Currents of Enchantment

Waves of colors splash in the breeze,
As the trees giggle among honeybees.
A rainbow slips on a pair of bright shoes,
Dancing in puddles too joyous to lose.

Frogs in tuxedos sing songs of delight,
While fireflies twinkle like stars in the night.
The river hums tunes made of butter and cream,
As fish hold a feast on a bubblegum dream.

A canvas of giggles with brushes that play,
Splashing and splattering clouds of bright gray.
Whiskers of kittens plot silly escapes,
On bicycles made of swirls and of shapes.

In a vibrant display of enchantment's embrace,
Colors conspire to tickle and race.
With laughter they flow, as joyous as day,
In this whimsical world where fun leads the way.

Echoes of Infinite Dimensions

In a realm where cats can fly,
Bananas roll, and donuts sigh.
Time bends like silly putty,
Everyone's a little nutty.

Jellybeans rain from the sky,
Dancing frogs pass by.
Wormholes lead to pizza shops,
Where every slice has funny hops.

Gravity is just a joke,
And spacetime likes to choke.
Brave the maze of silly dreams,
Giggles bounce like playful beams.

So come, dear friend, explore with glee,
In this zany place, wild and free.
Where laughter echoes through the halls,
And nonsense reigns, with joy that sprawls.

Whispers in the Fourth Realm

In the fourth realm, shadows tease,
Ticklish whispers on the breeze.
Clouds are made of candy fluff,
And butterflies are quite the tough.

Galaxies waltz in silly shoes,
Jellyfish sing the evening blues.
Mice wear hats and dance on stars,
While turtles cruise in tiny cars.

Banters bounce like rubber balls,
As gravity takes fun-filled falls.
Laughter echoes, far and wide,
In this realm, joy's the guide.

So step inside and join the fun,
Where every day's a whirling run.
With giggles shared in cosmic roars,
Adventure calls from endless shores.

Fractured Stories of Cosmic Journeys

Once a star tried to wear a hat,
But it only ended flat.
Comets chased a wobbly moon,
While shadow puppets played a tune.

Nebulae played hide and seek,
Shining bright, but far too meek.
A penguin danced upon a beam,
In a spacetime giggle dream.

Aliens dined on purple stew,
Swapping jokes, both old and new.
Quarks were bouncing off the wall,
With quantum fizz—and that's not all!

Through fractures bright, the tales unwind,
Chasing humor that's well-defined.
Join the parade of cosmic cheer,
For laughter is the language here.

The Multiverse Chronicles

In a universe made of cheese,
Bouncing brie brings everyone to knees.
Galaxies of grilled cheese beams,
Floating along in buttered dreams.

Dimensions swirl like fruity drinks,
Superheroes with funny winks.
A rabbit drives a cosmic ride,
With jellybeans as his guide.

Time trips on a rubber band,
While socks revolt and take a stand.
Wormholes lead to funny places,
Where laughter fills all the spaces.

So spin and twirl through all the realms,
With giggles steering at the helms.
In this multiverse, wild and vast,
The chuckles and joy are meant to last.

The Lattice of Lost Memories

In webs of spun recall, I trip,
Forgotten socks that make me slip.
The clock is stuck, it goes to no place,
As memories dance in a comical space.

A cat in a hat sings out loud,
While I search for the pants that I once vowed.
Each laugh echoes in corners dark,
As I stumble through like an awkward shark.

The fridge hums tunes from days of yore,
Offering snacks I cannot ignore.
Spoon and spork, a fork in the way,
How did my best lunch turn out this way?

Jellybeans bounce, oh what a mess,
Life's puzzle pieces, a jigsaw guess.
In every lost moment, I find a grin,
In the lattice where chaos begins.

Constellations of Forgotten Realities

Stars twinkle wildly, their dance out of sync,
As I ponder the mysteries of the fridge's stink.
Planets of pizza spin in the void,
Reality flips, but I'm far from annoyed.

UFOs made of tin can fly,
With aliens who wear silly ties.
Galaxies swirl in a comical jest,
Where no one seems to know what is best.

Asteroids shaped like socks and shoes,
In this cosmic riddle, I can't refuse.
I float on a thought, I whirl in delight,
As laughter ignites in the middle of night.

Constellations giggle, stars nod with glee,
Mapping out worlds where odd is the key.
In this vast space where quirks like to lay,
I find joy in the bizarre of the day.

Dimensions in Dissonance

In one realm, I'm a marvel of grace,
In the next, I trip over my shoelace.
Beating drums of a crazy parade,
Where dancing elephants lead the charade.

A toaster sings ballads, a blender croons,
While cats jump through hoops made of spoons.
Each corner turns into a whimsical stage,
Where nonsense rules in this colorful page.

I leap into dreams, I twist and I twirl,
Finding myself in a fizzy whirl.
Standing tall, then shrinking down small,
The rhythm of life, a kooky free-for-all.

In this dimension, we all break the mold,
Where laughter is treasure and stories unfold.
So tiptoe through puns, let your worries disperse,
In the dissonance found, we all can converse.

Pathways of the Paradox

Two roads diverged, both paths are wild,
One leads to chaos, the other, a child.
With shoes made of jelly and hats made of cheese,
I ponder realities made to appease.

A riddle of riddles, a quest for a snack,
In the maze of desires, I lose my track.
Forks in the road play peek-a-boo,
While giggles emerge from the skies so blue.

Through silly realms where dreams like to tick,
I chase after laughter, it's quite a trick.
With bouncing umbrellas adorned with intent,
I shuffle along, on this path that's so bent.

Paradoxes dance like bees in a swarm,
Creating a weather unlike any norm.
So join in the fun, let's twist and entangle,
In the pathways we stroll, where giggles wrangle.

Spectrum of Shattered Realms

In a realm where colors clash,
Red and blue begin to splash.
A yellow cat, with shoes so tight,
Dances under neon light.

A curious dog in a funky bow,
Says, "Let's race, but take it slow!"
They trip on rainbows, land in a pie,
While laughing at clouds up in the sky.

Ninjas made of cheese fly around,
Mice in capes, a sight profound!
A jester juggles bouncing stars,
While a pig plays tunes on brand new guitars.

Just a world of whimsy and cheer,
Where everything's more than it appears.
Join the dance, partake in the spree,
In this thought-bending comedy!

The Fabric of Fractal Wonders

In a quilt stitched with dreams so fine,
A snail rides a turtle's spine.
Mice make muffins in crooked hats,
While cats play chess with elaborate mats.

A strange professor with glasses askew,
Invents a gadget that cooks hot stew.
But be wary, it might fizz and pop,
Creating marshmallows that just won't stop.

Fractals dance in a dizzy swirl,
As the world flips—a twirling whirl!
Squirrels in capes zoom past the trees,
Chasing acorns with giggles and wheezes.

Let's toast to the quirks we all share,
In this fabric, enriched with flair.
Join the fun, don't be shy,
Lost in wonder, let's fly high!

Celestial Songs in the Void

Stars are singing a cosmic tune,
While comets dance and spin like a cartoon.
A moonbeam giggles, shines so bright,
As planets play hopscotch in the night.

The old sun winks, with a grin so wide,
Making space a fun-filled ride.
Aliens bake cakes from fluffy dust,
In a league where friendship is a must.

Supernovas throw dizzying light,
As asteroids form a conga line, tight.
Galactic berries bounce on a stem,
Sending waves of joy back to them.

What a place to picnic and play,
Under the stars, we'll dream away.
Join this cosmic, quirky parade,
In the void, our laughs cascade!

The Puzzles of Parallel Pathways

Two paths meet at a quirky fork,
Where shadows dance and rainbows talk.
One path leads to a land of cheese,
The other to gardens that giggle with bees.

A rabbit in glasses solves riddles profound,
While a squirrel spins tales all around.
They argue 'bout pie and the best kind of cake,
And try not to laugh as the earth starts to shake.

Sideways trees wear hats, so grand,
Each telling secrets, a jumbled band.
Step left, step right—what's the way home?
In whimsical realms, we freely roam.

So let's be silly, in this zestful maze,
Where puzzles delight and laughter plays.
Join the fun, let's dance a spell,
In parallel spaces, all is well!

Lightyears in a Whisper

In a galaxy's giggle, stars collide,
Silly comets dance on a cosmic slide.
Gravity's a prankster, don't take it to heart,
Black holes are just where shy stars depart.

Nebulas chuckle, glowing bright,
Planets play hide and seek, what a sight!
Asteroids toss confetti, a playful display,
Wormholes are portals to a timeless café.

Astro-bunnies hop through the lunar path,
Tickled by rockets, they giggle and laugh.
Lightyears mean nothing when fun's on a quest,
Just keep your arms up; it's an interstellar jest!

So swing with the moons and twirl with the sun,
In this vast, wacky universe, we're all here for fun.
Forget all the science, embrace the absurd,
Life's just a joke in the laughter of stars.

The Codex of Cosmic Crossroads

Do you hear the whispers of stars in a rush?
Galactic hitchhikers, in giggles they crush.
They argue and bicker on an astral street,
Trading old jokes that never skip a beat.

Cosmic chronicles scribbled in space,
Every quasar winks with a smile on its face.
Parallel pals sharing punchlines at bars,
Exchanging their tales in the light of the stars.

Nebulae named after quirky old kings,
Who wore flashy capes and danced with strings.
In this wild library of unwritten lore,
You never know what the next chapter stores.

So flip through the pages with a chuckle and grin,
In the cosmos' library, there's fun to begin.
Laugh out the worries, let curiosity roam,
In the codex of crossroads, we all find a home.

Echoing Dreams from Astral Roots

In the cradle of stardust, dreams take flight,
Bubbles of laughter in the velvet night.
Quasars tell stories with humor so sly,
Winking at planets as they float by.

Singing space whales with silly old tunes,
Filling the cosmos with giggles and swoons.
Meteor showers wear party hats tall,
As they crash down, making wishes for all.

Whirling through worlds where the odd traits align,
Time-traveling turtles sip bubbles of wine.
In the echo of laughter, we twist and we spin,
Finding joy in the chaos, letting the fun in.

So soar through the cosmos, where laughter runs free,
With stars as your mentors, you will see.
Dream big and bright, let your spirit elate,
For in the vast universe, joy is our fate.

Reveries in the Quantum Shift

In the dance of the atoms, tickles abound,
Particles jitter, grinning all around.
Schrodinger's cat is a comedian too,
Half in, half out, just pulling a coup.

Quantum leaps in socks, mismatched with glee,
Teleporting kittens with curious decree.
Looping in circles, a time-warped surprise,
All while the universe just rolls its eyes.

Through the wormholes of whimsy, we giggle and play,
Where every odd quantum can go its own way.
Frolicking photons with bright shining grins,
Join in the laughter as our adventure begins.

So wiggle your quarks and shimmy that spin,
In the vastness of silliness, we all dive in.
With glee at the forefront, let's warp into fun,
In the realm of the quirky, we're never outrun.

Shadows in a Shimmering Prism

In a land where shadows play,
Colors dance, then drift away.
A jellybean sky with candy trees,
As ducks in tuxedos say 'quack' with ease.

A quarter moon just dropped a shoe,
While giggling stars chant, 'How do you do?'
With wobbly waves in a lollipop sea,
All the silly creatures shout, 'Come see me!'

The sun wears socks, too bright to miss,
The clouds debate on who's the best fish.
With rainbows painted on cheeky grins,
Here, laughter's the only rule that wins.

So step right in, don't be shy,
In a prism world where giggles fly.
Your shadow might just pull a prank,
And all the colors will laugh and tank!

Dreams of Twisting Pathways

On twisting paths where socks roam free,
Umbrellas chatter in a giggly spree.
With cobblestones made of bubble gum,
Each step you take goes 'pop' like fun!

Chasing dreams on a roller-skate,
Penguins wobble; can't be late!
A teacup spins with biscuits bright,
While cats in hats play hide and bite.

A jester jumps on a pogo stick,
While clocks go backwards, playing tricks.
Imagining paths made of jellybeans,
We laugh loudly—oh, what silly scenes!

So dance with joy on a pathway strange,
With every step, let reality change.
In dreams of twist where giggles abound,
Playtime adventures will surely be found!

Flights Through Celestial Labyrinths

Through cosmic mazes of bouncy light,
Planets dodge, avoiding a fight.
With unicorns riding meteor showers,
They sprinkle joy like interstellar flowers.

A space cat dons the captain's hat,
As aliens dance with a friendly spat.
With comets racing for a hug,
They twirl and whirl like a dance in a mug.

Starry laughter fills the immense void,
Creating dreams that can't be destroyed.
In a world where gravity is just a joke,
We bounce on stars and explore, awoke!

So join the flight through wacky streams,
In labyrinths where nothing's as it seems.
With each twist and turn, joy's on display,
A funny journey that leads the way!

Mesmerizing Worlds Between Worlds

In a space where giggles blend and twist,
Clouds draped in candy, a minty mist.
Where jellyfish float under lemon trees,
And flowers play tag in a dance of ease.

Between two worlds, the laughter grows,
With colorful paths that nobody knows.
A toast with toast and a wink from a mouse,
Inside a cupcake that's also a house.

With snickering rabbits and winking stars,
They ride on bicycles made from Mars.
An orchestra of silliness fills the air,
As giggling gnomes sprout everywhere!

So come explore this chaotic delight,
In worlds between worlds, everything's bright.
With every tickle, the fun gets unfurled,
Embrace the madness of this funny world!

Songs from the Quantum Abyss

In a realm where cats can dance,
And socks form friendships by chance,
Chickens wear ties, toast in hand,
Jellybeans rule this bizarre land.

Tea with robots, such a delight,
They argue over who's more bright,
The sun wears shades, the moon plays chess,
While furniture joins in, feels no stress.

Unicorns croon to the starry night,
As waffles take off in their flight,
Numerous ducks quack with a tune,
Under the watch of a smiling moon.

Join the fun in this wondrous space,
Where giggles and grins fill every place,
Through wormholes, we skip, we spin and twirl,
In the quantum abyss, life's a whirl.

Between the Lines of Existence

Between the lines, the jokes unfold,
Where squirrels are bankers, stories told,
A cheese wheel rolls through the cosmic door,
And plants are gossiping, wanting more.

Aliens wear hats, capes in the sky,
Dropping off pizza as they fly by,
While shadows chat with the light of dawn,
A riddle that giggles, never withdrawn.

Bubblegum thoughts float around so sweet,
With rubber ducks dancing, offbeat,
Clocks tick backward, and everyone laughs,
Time's just a jest—nothing it halves.

In this playful world, we twirl and bend,
Life's just a jest, with no real end,
Between the lines, where laughter shines,
Existence tickles with endless designs.

The Geometry of Ghosts

In corners where the whispers dwell,
Ghosts juggle numbers, cast a spell,
Hexagons trip on spectral beams,
While triangles plot their daring schemes.

Curves have parties, right angles swoon,
Under the light of a puzzling moon,
Chasing reflections—a raucous race,
In this ghostly, geometric space.

The numbers giggle, twist, and shout,
As poltergeists waltz all about,
Spooky shapes with a silly grin,
Join in the fun, let the laughter begin.

In angles of mirth, they swirl and spin,
Finding joy where the laughter's been,
The geometry here is truly a boast,
As we dance with the quirky, lively ghosts.

Visions of the Nebulae

In the depths of space, where dreams collide,
The nebulae laugh, they don't need to hide,
They sing to the stars with a playful cheer,
While comets throw parties, bringing good beer.

With galaxies spinning like tops in a game,
And quasars bursting, igniting the flame,
Asteroids dance in their dazzling spree,
While planets stack up for a cosmic tea.

Puppies in orbit, chasing their tails,
Jovial laughter across the trails,
In the vacuum where starlight gleams,
The universe chuckles, bursting with dreams.

So join the ride through this playful space,
In visions of nebulae, find your place,
Where the cosmos giggles and dances bright,
In the vastness of humor, endless delight.

Portals to Potentialities

In cracks of space, we squirrel and dart,
With socks mismatched, we play our part.
Each door that swings, a goofy chance,
To waltz with fate in a quirky dance.

We're whisked away on carts of cream,
A whirlwind ride, a loony dream.
Tea with llamas and giggling cats,
Oh, the oddity of those acrobats!

With hats like cakes and shoes of cheese,
Every venture prompts a laugh with ease.
Bouncing off the walls, we find our beat,
Where giggles echo, life's a treat.

So grab a ticket to the absurd,
In realms of nonsense, bliss is stirred.
Run through portals, let laughter swell,
In sparkly places, all is well!

Dreams Interlaced with Light

Whispers of starlight sprinkle the ground,
In dreams of jellybeans, joy is found.
We ride on rainbows, slide on clouds,
With chuckles booming, we laugh aloud.

A squirrel in pajamas plays the piano,
While dancing stars join in the show.
Bubblegum rivers flow silky and bright,
As we frolic and twirl in pure delight.

The moon wears spectacles, grinning wide,
A cosmic circus, with unicorns to ride.
With every turn, a giggle escapes,
In lands where zany magic reshapes.

So snuggle up, let the dreams ignite,
In this wild realm, everything's right.
Together we'll travel by glittering flight,
In the soft embrace of dreams alight.

Navigating the Nexus of Now

In this twisty maze, we skip and hop,
With garden gnomes and lollipops.
Time dances silly, all jumbled and bright,
Every moment's a joke, pure delight!

Wormholes swirl with belly laughs,
Clocks play tricks, cutting time in halves.
We chase the giggles in loops and whirls,
As marshmallow balloons float and twirl.

Bouncing from one jest to the next,
In this goofy realm, we feel perplexed.
The air is thick with laughter's glow,
It's now or never, come steal the show!

So grab your friends, let's twinkle and spin,
In the nexus where the fun begins.
Every tick of the clock, a raucous cheer,
Here in the now, there's naught to fear!

Patterns in the Cosmic Whirl

Stars wear hats shaped like croissants,
A cosmic jig, a dance that flaunts.
With jellyfish joined in the merry swirl,
Patterns emerge in a giggly whirl.

Gravity's a prankster with clownish flair,
As we twirl through universes, light as air.
With bouncing beans and popping fizz,
Every loop and twist, pure cosmic whizz!

A kaleidoscope of whimsy and fun,
Chasing comets, making puns.
Here colors giggle, and shapes rejoice,
In this funny place, let's raise our voice.

So laugh with me in this cosmic spree,
Where laughter spins wild and carefree.
In patterns bright, let's jump and twirl,
Amidst the chaos, we find our pearl!

Threads of Temporal Tapestry

In a world where socks often disappear,
Time giggles with a cheeky sneer.
Wormholes hide my missing shoes,
As I dance through paradoxes and trivial clues.

Tick-tock goes my playful clock,
Chasing moments like a tricky flock.
I step on epochs, trip on a sigh,
Laughter echoes as days slip by.

Oh look, there's a cat in a top hat,
Riding a unicorn, imagine that!
We juggle time like it's a game,
Where nothing is quite the same.

In the threads of fate, garments unwind,
Wearing mismatched socks is well defined.
Each stitch tells a tale of surprise,
In my closet, the universe lies.

The Enigma of the Elusive Edge

What's at the end? A paradox, I bet,
A squirrel in shades, or a talking pet?
The edge of reality is funny and sly,
Where ducks wear bowties and pigs learn to fly.

I tiptoe to wisdom with a rubber chicken,
Every riddle's a giggle, and I'm never stricken.
The wisdom of ages in jellybeans hides,
As the universe chuckles with comical strides.

Wormholes open into a ball pit,
Gravity's a prankster, not to be outwit.
Dance with dimensions, twirl with delight,
Forget about logic, let's party tonight!

The riddle's resolved with flip-flop flair,
Where clock hands wave as if they don't care.
With laughter as my guiding thread,
I leap through the edges where nothing is said.

Reverberations in the Cosmic Silence

Stars giggle softly in the deep, dark sky,
Bubbles of laughter as galaxies sigh.
Invisible pranks by the moonlight play,
Tangles of humor in the Milky Way.

Whispers of echoes from comets on cue,
Tickling the orbits as they twirl and skew.
Solar winds carry a whimsical tune,
As planets spin tales from morning till noon.

In the void where space decides to prank,
Meteors slide down the cosmic flank.
Playful rhythms bring joy near and far,
As I dance on a comet, a cosmic star.

Oh snap! A black hole just swallowed my sock,
Time and space giggle, what a great shock!
In the silence of space, laughter is bound,
As the universe spins with joy all around.

Silhouettes of Timelessness

Shadows dance whimsically in the light,
Time stands still, but oh, what a sight!
With sneakers and tophats, they stroll in style,
Inventing new moves that'll make you smile.

An hourglass squirts sand like confetti,
While clocks spin a tale that's more than petty.
Waltzing with whimsy, we slip and slide,
On the timeline's edge, we gleefully ride.

The past wears polka dots, the future, stripes,
Every moment a canvas, where laughter types.
Echoes of giggles bounce off the stars,
In silhouettes of timelessness, we erase our scars.

With every tick, we riff and rhyme,
Find the humor hidden in every crime.
These moments are fleeting, but they're so grand,
In the dance of existence, let's take a stand.

Mapping the Ethereal Expanse

In a realm where socks disappear,
Maps of fun chaos always near.
Dancing about in zero-grav,
Laughing shadows, bold and brash.

Who knew that time had a silly rhyme?
Wobbling giggles join the climb.
Cards and crayons in space collide,
As cosmic doodles take a ride.

Bouncing off the walls with flair,
Invisible brushes brush the air.
With each mistake, a comet's tail,
Painting nonsense on the scale.

Lines get crossed and chaos reigns,
In a world where humor gains.
Maps unravel, spirit's delight,
In the expanse, oh what a sight!

Journey to the Heart of the Continuum

A journey starts with a silly quirk,
Through the loops where the giggles lurk.
Past the clouds that wobble and sway,
Finding joy in the odd ballet.

Through portals lined with rubber bands,
Time tickles with clownish hands.
Finding treasures in the void's caprice,
Each twist and turn, a whispered fleece.

Dancing neurons in a crazy loop,
Riding comets on a spiraling stoop.
Heartbeats sync with laughter's song,
In the continuum, we all belong.

Here's to moments that feel so strange,
Where everyday norms start to change.
With each weird step, a chance we take,
In this dance, make no mistake!

The Silence Between the Stars

In the quiet of space, a whisper flies,
Full of mischief and silly sighs.
Stars snicker, hiding behind their glow,
Giggles echo where no one can go.

Between the twinkles, pranks arise,
A cosmic joke that never dies.
Asteroids chuckle, comets grin,
As silence wraps us deep within.

Nebulas spin in jolly hues,
With secrets shared like old-time news.
In this quiet, mischief reigns,
Sending chuckles through the cosmic lanes.

Catch a laugh e'en from a star,
Who'd think silence could go that far?
In the depths of dark, there's fun to weave,
A tapestry of joy we believe!

Fragments of Chronological Color

Scattered pieces of time's own art,
Colors burst like laughs to impart.
Purple polka dots and yellow swirls,
A canvas of chaos, a dance unfurls.

Chronicles painted with giddy strokes,
Time's whispers emerge as cheerful jokes.
Fragments wiggle and flit around,
In this rainbow realm, joy is found.

A tick-tock twist, a laugh with grace,
Colors collide in a playful race.
With each new shade, giggles ignite,
Turning history into pure delight.

So gather the splatters, splash them wide,
In the gallery of time, let laughter glide.
Each hue a memory, a joy to hold,
A funny story, forever told!

Enigmatic Entrances to Elsewhere

A door with no handle, oh what a sight,
It twists and it turns, just out of light.
Don't touch the frame, there's a sign: 'Beware!',
Is that a cat, or a dog over there?

A window that giggles, it laughs right out loud,
It opens to nowhere, you know it's not proud.
It shifts like a wave, so playful, so spry,
Look quick, it just winked - or was that a lie?

Steps made of jelly, they bounce when you tread,
You'd think they were bouncing, but oh no, they fled.
The floor's a trampoline, up and down we go,
Catch me if you can, but we've nowhere to flow!

We gather our socks, to chase after dreams,
But socks always vanish - or so it seems.
With giggles and chuckles, we skip through the panes,
In a world where logic simply unchains.

Portents of a Polychromatic Journey

A map made of candy, it's sticky and sweet,
Follow the colors, a rainbow retreat.
But beware of the gumdrops, they bite at your toes,
While licorice rivers will tangle your clothes.

The traveler's hat spins, it's lost in the wind,
It talks about places where time is a whim.
"I once met a squirrel who danced in a tree,
He wore shiny boots and invited me."

At every turn, whispering clouds start to chime,
"Take the left fork and you'll dance with some lime!"
But what is a lime? Is it truly a fruit?
Or perhaps one of those small dancing boots?

Each step is a chuckle, the grass turns to bread,
You can feast on your journey and nap when you're fed.
In this land of the silly, everything's bright,
May your laughter be sweet, and your worries take flight!

Mirage of the Dimensional Door

A door made of bubbles, it sparkles and gleams,
It leads to a place where reality beams.
Come join a parade of the odd and the fun,
With elephants twirling and kangaroos run!

The handle's a pickle, it squeaks when you turn,
"Enter," it whispers, "where dreams twist and burn!"
But don't mind the fire, it's friendly, you see,
It cooks up a storm of sweet jelly for tea.

A wall made of giggles will tickle your toes,
With shadows that dance and the silliness flows.
A rainbow of whispers, they tickle your ear,
Each word is a tickle, it's laughter you hear.

In a realm full of chaos, where nonsense is king,
The wind plays a tune, and the blind mice can sing.
So step through the portal, leap into the glee,
Where bubbles and laughter are wild and set free!

The Sphere of Shared Realities

Imagine a bubble that floats in the air,
Each breath that we take, it giggles with flair.
Three cheers for the universe, wild and absurd,
Where even the birds have their own funny verb.

A teapot made of laughter, it whistles a tune,
With flavors of mayhem, it brews a cartoon.
Pour in a smile, sip joy when you can,
But mind the cranky old cat, he's part of the plan.

A merry-go-round spins a plot thick as fog,
With mirrors reflecting a clownish old dog.
"Oh, where are we going?" the hedgehog does ask,
"To the land of the silly, behind a light mask."

So frolic with friends, in this peculiar sphere,
Where absurdity's rampant, and jokes are quite near.
With shared silly moments, we float and we play,
In realms of pure laughter, come seize the day!

Interwoven Stories of Space

Once a comet lost its path,
Swirled around in cosmic baths,
It bumped a star, created glee,
That star said, "Hey! You're bumping me!"

A black hole slipped on cosmic ice,
Sucked in a planet, thought it was nice,
"What a meal!" it chuckled a bit,
But it burped, and then the planet split.

Next up, asteroids threw a dance,
In zero-gravity, they took a chance,
With funky moves, they twirled in lines,
A space rave with no earthly signs.

Thus, the universe loves to jest,
Laughs with quarks, at its very best,
In this grand play, so light and spry,
Stars wink, and asteroids fly high.

Chronicles of the Celestial Grid

In the grid where space-time bends,
Sat a quasar with cosmic friends,
They cracked jokes about light years,
And drank stardust, filled with cheers.

A neutron star wore a party hat,
Twirled around, and then—splat!—
It tried to dance, but oh dear me,
Ended up stuck in a cosmic tree.

Planets played hide and seek all night,
Twirling moons filled with delight,
One hid behind a ring of dust,
But was found—so much for trust.

The cosmic web, a tangled play,
Brings laughter in its quirky way,
For in this realm, we find such bliss,
Even stardust can't resist the giggles.

The Unfolding of Hidden Mazes

In a maze of stars, a snail strolled slow,
Lost in thought as black holes glowed,
It turned a corner, spoke with flair,
"I'm just here for the cosmic air!"

Wormholes whispered, "This way or that!"
A spacetime twist—a cosmic spat,
One worm grinned, the other frowned,
And laughter echoed all around.

Tangled paths with giggles that rung,
Constellations danced, their tales were sung,
Twinkling giggles flashed through the night,
As wandering comets sparkled bright.

So here we find a cosmic jest,
In the fractals, they laugh the best,
For even in mazes, lost and free,
Joy unfolds in a galaxy spree.

Mirages in the Kaleidoscope

Through a kaleidoscope, I peeked one day,
Saw a planet wear a coat of clay,
It wobbled and jiggled, so out of place,
"Don't judge me!" it cried, "I'm on my own space!"

Stars twinkled back in mischievous glee,
"Meet our friends, the funny debris!"
With laughter erupting, they formed a band,
Echoed across the vast, cosmic land.

Saturn danced in its glittering rings,
Winking joy at all the silly things,
A meteor shower joined the tune,
Bouncing and bursting like a cartoon.

In this mirage, the cosmos shines bright,
Filled with giggles, a playful delight,
For in each twist and colorful lore,
Laughter's the language, forevermore.

Navigating the Labyrinth of Light

In a maze made of beams so bright,
I tripped on a shadow, oh what a sight!
A squirrel with a map, wearing a tie,
Said, 'Follow me, or you'll surely die!'

The walls were sparkling, the floors like stars,
I danced with the beams, forgot about cars.
A jellybean monster offered me cake,
But only if I could swim in a lake!

Every corner turned, a giggle would sprout,
What strange things to see when you wander about!
A pizza slice spoke, 'What's your quest?'
In a labyrinth of light, I'm just here for the jest!

So I chuckled through corridors, graceful and wide,
With giggles and sparkles, I took it in stride.
In every reflection, a riddle to find,
In a labyrinth of light, I'm a curious kind!

Harmonies of the Fourth Layer

In the fourth layer, music takes flight,
A poodle in shades sings every night.
With rubber duck choirs and foxes on drums,
Each note brings laughter as laughter just hums.

The walls are made of marshmallow sound,
Echoes of giggles in wholes all around.
A saxophone fish sways to the beat,
While penguins tap dance with flippers so neat!

I found my lost socks, they formed a band,
With startles and chuckles, it's quite unplanned.
Each layer I climb, the laughter gets loud,
As quirky musicians gather a crowd!

So we sway and we croon, in a whimsical haze,
In harmonies strange, lost in the maze.
Every chuckle climbs higher, twirls through the air,
In the fourth layer's party, no reason to care!

The Riddles of Recursive Realities

In a mirror that giggles, oh what a sight,
Reflections of me talking left and right.
'What's the best way to travel?' I ask to a chair,
'Sit down and spin, you'll float through the air!'

Two cats in top hats whisper behind,
'Where does the sun go? It leaves when it's kind.'
I ponder and ponder, it's quite a surprise,
As ducks in bowties do try to advise.

Each riddle I hear, it loops in my brain,
So I follow a snail who dances in rain.
They say every question holds wonders untold,
So I laugh at the riddles, my heart turns to gold!

Through recursive paths that twist and that twine,
I chase all the puzzles, I stumble, I shine.
With each quirky answer, joy's like confetti,
In the chaos of riddles, I'm always quite ready!

Enchanted Byways of Existence

Down the path of whimsy, I took a long stroll,
Past fairies on bicycles, dusting the shoal.
With giggles and grins, they waved me on through,
'The more that you laugh, the more fun you'll accrue!'

A bent tree in glasses said 'What's your desire?'
I answered 'To dance in a cake-popping choir!'
So the stars in the sky clapped their twinkling hands,
As marching marshmallows danced in their bands.

The rainbow-topped hedgehog spun tales of delight,
While jellyfish jived in the heart of the night.
The enchanted byways twinkled and glowed,
With giggles and dreams, the laughter just flowed!

So I skipped through dimensions, a grin plastered wide,
With blossoms of mirth dancing right at my side.
In pathways of magic where nonsense rules king,
Every step I take feels like a joyful spring!

Whispers Beyond the Veil

In a land where socks go to hide,
Washing machines spin tales with pride.
They dance with lint on a cosmic stage,
Laughing at time, like a playful sage.

A cat in a hat with four tiny legs,
Juggles the sun while sipping on eggs.
With whiskers aglow, he starts to sing,
Of mischief and magic, oh what a thing!

A frog in a bowtie leaps through the air,
Chasing his dreams with whimsical flair.
He lands on a lily, gives a grand cheer,
Knowing the universe holds no fear.

So giggle and chuckle, don't take a peek,
At the odd little quirks of the time-twisted week.
With whimsy and wonders that never grow stale,
We find our delight in whispers beyond the veil.

Fragments of a Fractal Dream

In a dream where the pancakes are stacked so high,
A squirrel in a vest claims he can fly.
He flips them with flair, a culinary feat,
While the syrup flows like a river of sweet.

A turtle in sneakers races a hare,
They tied their shoelaces with whimsical flair.
In circles they run, both meek and bold,
Chasing their tails, a sight to behold.

The fish wear top hats and dance on the sand,
As bubbles rise up with a tickle at hand.
They giggle and gurgle, all caught in a stream,
These beautiful chaos, fragments of a dream.

So come take a stroll on this playful spree,
Where laughter and lightness flow wild and free.
In patterns that twist, where joy's the main theme,
We revel together in a fractal dream.

Journeys Through the Hypercube

A hamster in glasses reads a thick book,
On how to fly kites with a wide-open hook.
He launches his dreams to the great unknown,
In a world where the weird is perfectly grown.

A porcupine chef bakes pizzas with glee,
Each slice holds a mystery, like a dance of the sea.
With toppings that giggle and cheese that can sing,
He serves up a slice of a marvelous thing.

A goldfish in orbit dreams of the ground,
While riding a comet that never slows down.
They swirl through the stars, a dizzying flight,
Turning physics to laughter, from dark into light.

In corners of cosmos, where oddities fuse,
We find joy in journeys, no paths to refuse.
With giggles and puzzles, we play without hues,
In the vastness of wonder through the hypercube's views.

Shadows of the Multiverse

In a realm where shadows play leapfrog at night,
A pirate with polka dots sails into sight.
His ship's made of candy, full of choco treasure,
He laughs with the moon, what a whimsical pleasure!

A wizard's hat drifts on a cloud made of pie,
As dragons serve tea, all scampering by.
With biscuits that float and spoons that can dance,
They stir up enchantment with every fun chance.

The garden of giggles blooms flowers of jest,
Where jokes grow like veggies, each one is a quest.
They tickle the skunks and make rainbows of cheer,
Painting smiles on faces, magic so near.

So peek into shadows where laughter is rife,
Embrace the absurd, it's the joy of our life.
In this whimsical world, where laughter can burst,
We celebrate wonders, the shadows of the multiverse.

www.ingramcontent.com/pod-product-compliance
Lightning Source LLC
Chambersburg PA
CBHW072214070526
44585CB00015B/1330